A Magic Manual to turn your
Dreams to **Destiny**

SO BE IT!

from **Where you are**

to **Where you want to be...**

KALYANI HARIHARAN

I dedicate this book to my parents **Ramadurai** and *(Late)* **Meenakshi** and my in-laws *(Late)* **Viswanathan** and **Swarnam**, who have shaped me in many ways, with their presence.

To all my fellow travelers of life, who dare to dream and create their own Destiny.

GRATITUDE

This is going to be quite a list but has to be said.

People come into your life for a reason, a season or a lifetime. The following people are my all-season souls and have stayed with me through fair and foul weather.

My immense gratitude to my husband Hariharan, who has always supported me and encouraged me to dream and create my own destiny and picked me up many times, when I fell down and doubted myself. He has been a pillar of strength and faith. Thank you, Hari.

To my sons Prahaladh and Parikshith who constantly pushed me to pursue my dreams and had faith in my capabilities, even when I felt that I was just good to be a stay- at- home mom.

To my brothers Rajesh and Anand and my sisters-in-law Lalitha, Radhika, Minu and Krithika and my brothers in law, Jayaraman and Viswanathan- my cheerleaders.

To the newest entrant into my life - My sweet and talented daughter-in-law Sruthakeerthy, who read my first draft and gave valuable inputs (I know she had no other choice ☺)

To my bestie Aldrin Edwards, my partner in crime, who helps me to explore and establish all my hair-brained schemes and ideas and betters them in executing them. He has painstakingly helped me in editing this book from A-Z. For a non-reader, he has done a fabulous job. Thank you, Aldrin.

To my earthly guardian angel Peter Paul who edited the first draft of this book and added valuable insights. He remains my sounding board for all my desires and dreams and helps me in reaching my goals faster with his unwavering faith, love and guidance.

To Murali Sundaram, founder of TLC (Teachers Leaders Community), through whom I was encouraged to become an author and release this book under their umbrella. Thank you, Murali, Guna and team, for your consistent encouragement.

To my mentor Siddharth Rajsekar, founder of Internet Lifestyle Hub, who has created his own destiny and is helping millions of people create their own destiny. He is a Digital Guru par excellence and I owe so much to him. He inspires me. Thank you Sidz.

To my two adorable pets, Precious and Popeye, who keep me absolutely grounded (literally, as I can't step out☺)

Above all I thank myself and this wonderful Universe for guiding me to dream and create my own destiny. For leaving me clues everywhere as signs and helping me to read them. For sending people in my life and for the life experiences through them. For helping me bounce back and understand my own power.

Advance gratitude to the readers and action takers, who want to create their own destiny.

With Immense Love and Gratitude,

Kalyani

<u>CONTENTS</u>

CASTLES IN THE AIR

Picture this. It is 1977.

Place – The City of Joy, Calcutta (currently Kolkata).

In a small 300 sq. ft. home, a young girl, lived with her two younger brothers, grand-parents and parents. Happy, tom-boyish, boisterous, two long pigtails (the ends plaited with colored ribbons which she hated) and with not a care in the world, she had this habit of voicing out aloud her teeniest desires/dreams and aspirations. No. There were no goal setting workshops those days. But people around used to ask this famously infamous question, "What will you become when you grow up?" A question which flummoxes young ones, even today. Not everyone knows what they want to do in life. And most parents did not feel it a need to drum it in their children's heads that they should become engineers or doctors. Though even back then, these were the most coveted jobs.

Well, this young girl in Calcutta had many varied answers to this singular question - depending on her mood 😊

Having read about Florence Nightingale, she wanted to be a nurse – full of compassion, dressing wounds and caring for the wounded.

At other times she wanted to be a doctor – saving lives, healing the sick.

But in a fancy-dress competition having dressed up as Mother Teresa, obviously she wanted to be like Mother Teresa, and uplift the poor.

She loved her English teacher and there were times she wanted to become a teacher and be loved and be kind to all the students – especially those who were weak in Mathematics. You see, she disliked numbers and still does. (She did become a English teacher and got over her fear of numbers by learning abacus)

She dreamt of living in a huge mansion, with frilly white lacy curtains, a garden with profuse flowers and a lawn, each room making a statement of its own, a room to call her own. She kept sketching layouts of houses in her own way. She didn't know about architects or buildings or civil engineering.

She wanted to be famous – a famous singer as she loved music. She wanted to teach music.

She wanted to be an author, an actor, an air- hostess, she desired to be a boy so that she would get the freedom that boys had. Her list was endless.

Her grandmother often chided her, to stop building 'Manakottai' (in Tamil, it means CASTLES IN THE AIR.)

She wishes her granny was alive today – so she could tell her that, the whole wide world is talking about *Visualization, Imagination* and asking for what you want, which plays a great role in manifesting one's desires. Building castles in the air can be the beginning of creating one's own reality.

And thus, continuing to be rich in her imagination about the endless possibilities of manifesting one's dreams and desires into one's chosen destiny, this Calcutta girl now a grown and worldly-wise woman, decided to create a guide, a lighthouse for all those who have either lost their deepest desires and dreams in the swirling seas of mundane existential living, or for those who never had any dreams or desires to begin with, in the form of this book you are reading at the moment.

SO BE IT! - is a self-help magic manual to guide you to turn your Dreams to Destiny and make your desires come true with the Laws of The Universe.

A dream is no frivolous term. Our aspirations are actually called dreams, because they are yet to be fulfilled. Dreams are the hopes for our future.

Dreams are nothing but our deep desires, waiting to be realized and become a reality. These are not the dreams that we experience when we sleep. These are dreams we see in our mind's eye when we are wide awake and filling our cognitive spaces. These are dreams which are with us all the time, silent and steady, just waiting to be acknowledged. These dreams or aspirations will not allow us to sleep, till we make them happen. These dreams are extremely personal and unique. These dreams lead to ambitions, goals and a purpose in life. They may play hide and seek, because of our individual life circumstances, but they continue to be in existence, nonetheless.

It can be a small desire like drinking that wonderful cup of coffee every day before the world wakes up, or the ability to enjoy the dance in the rain.

Or it can be huge dreams like wanting to create a business conglomerate and be the next Elon Musk or hold an empire like the Royalty of England. It doesn't matter as long as it is important to us, it fulfils our sense of mission and purpose in life, adds value to ourselves and others, and it brings happiness to all. It could be anything. Being a sportsperson to being a parent, a beloved child, a doctor or an actor or simply, being yourself. How do we take our dreams from our mind space and make it a reality, make it tangible? How do we create our own destiny?

This book is based on this famous quote which paves a path for us to follow our dreams in a systematic manner.

*Watch Your **THOUGHTS**,*
*they Become **WORDS**.*
*Watch your **WORDS**,*
*they Become **ACTIONS**.*
*Watch your **ACTIONS**,*
*they become **HABITS**.*
*Watch your **HABITS**,*
*they become your **CHARACTER**.*
*Watch your **CHARACTER**,*
*they become your **DESTINY**.*

> *"What we call our destiny is truly our character and that character can be altered. The knowledge that we are responsible for our actions and attitudes does not need to be discouraging, because it also means that we are free to change this destiny. One is not in bondage to the past, which has shaped our feelings, to race, inheritance, background. All this can be altered if we have the courage to examine how it formed us. We can alter the chemistry provided we have the courage to dissect the elements."*
>
> {Anais Nin, The Diary of Anaïs Nin, Vol. 1: 1931-1934}

Reinvent. Co-create. Chisel yourself. Be your own sculptor and sculpture. Change. Transform. Take the power into your own hands.

All you have to do is invest in yourself. In terms of energy, effort, intention, action and all the steps which will help you create your destiny. So, the big question here is - Can we even create our own destiny?

How do we create our own destiny? What is fate? Do we have control over our lives? Is it really possible to manifest what we want? All these questions and more are answered in this book. Experiences, Techniques, Tools, Principles and Laws of The Universe are shared here, with exercises and worksheets for you to follow and create your own destiny.

Much has been said, read, and written about creating our own destiny. It is a fascinating subject. One common thought we all have is the hand that fate or destiny has over us. Do we have any control or power over our own lives or is it all pre-determined? Sometimes, it all seems so fatalistic.

It could be God or Karma having power over us. There is this karmic cycle which decides our birth in this planet Earth. It is both. It is a question of chance and choice and pre - determined situations.

In the physical sense we did not choose our birth, parents, siblings, or challenges we are born with, born in poverty or royalty- these are not in our hands. In the spiritual sense, it is believed that the soul choses its own path and decides when and where to be born and to whom.

> *"We are not human beings having a spiritual experience; we are spiritual beings having a human experience."*
>
> **- Pierre Teilhard de Chardin**

But, if that is the case, why would we do anything to change our life? While the concept of Karma, Dharma and Fate have a hold on us, we are still given the power of choice, to live and create our lifestyle.

One can be born poor, but one need not live their entire life in poverty. There are thousands of live examples around us of people who have gone from rags to riches.

Destiny is futuristic whereas Fate is what has been given to us. Destiny also means that we have the power within us to make best use of what is handed over to us at birth. Astrological charts, tarot cards, palm-reading and likes are just predictions, not a reality. They are just sign-boards. If you believe in all this. Let us take an example.

While driving, you must have noticed that there are sign boards which reads, *"Curve Ahead", "Drive Slow", or "Accident Prone Zone"*. We could completely ignore the warning signs and drive casually or drive negligently in disregard of them, and there could be every possibility of an accident. It is only a prediction, not a reality. The choice is in our hands.

The power of CHOICE is so empowering.

Every human being has the power of his or her free-will and agency, that they can employ to dream, desire, direct their lives in the face of their individual life circumstances, and manifest their destiny. It could be in health, wealth, finance, career, love, relationships.

Creating your own destiny is a spiritual journey, looking inwards; a journey of self- awakening and living life to the fullest. It begins with identifying what you want in your life, the kind of lifestyle that you want, identifying your gifts and talents which each of you possess and matching them to create your own tapestry.

This book will traverse the path one can take to evolve your Desires and manifest your Destiny – From understanding Desire and Intent to thoughts and actions, leading to Habits and character building and finally to your Destiny. It has sub-chapters on Manifestation, Consistency, Implementation and Self-Transformation which will help you reach your goal.

Join me by reading this book, implement the tools and techniques, follow the process and let's celebrate your happiness and success and be part of the magic in your life – that YOU ARE GOING TO CREATE for yourself!

It is identifying and nurturing the gifts and talents that nature has bestowed upon you.

Your life is in your hands. Make it powerful, colourful and beautiful. You are Destiny's child. Go, create your world!

With Immense Love and Gratitude,

I remain yours,

Kalyani

<u>**Disclaimer:**</u> Do not buy this book if you think you do not have the power to create your own destiny. If you do not believe in yourself.

This book is for believers, for those who are willing to go through the grind to create their own destiny with the gifts that the Universe has bestowed on them.

And if you chance upon this book, maybe it's a message or sign from the universe that the time has now come for you to create your own destiny.

HOW TO READ THIS BOOK

This book is written in a letter format. I wrote this for you, my dear reader, whose happiness and success I so desire.

Each chapter begins with 'My Dearest ....' Take that pen and write your name in each chapter, after My Dearest – in Bold and Color. Personalize this book and start reading NOW.

It empowers me to see you EMPOWERED. Read, make notes, ponder, dig your dreams out, act on it and color the entire universe with your joy and wisdom and touch the lives of people.

1

The World of

Intention and Desire

(As You Wish)

The Law of Intention and Desire states that:

"Inherent in every intention and desire is the mechanics for its fulfillment. Intention and desire in the field of pure potentiality have infinite organizing power. And when we introduce an intention in the fertile ground of pure potentiality, we put this infinite organizing power to work for us."

- Deepak Chopra

The seven spiritual laws of success

"The discipline of desire is the background of character."

- John Locke

What you **"desire"** with focused **"intent"**, followed by **"actions to attain"** the object of your desire, is also the path to **"manifesting your destiny."**

"It sometimes seems that intense desire creates not only its own opportunities, but also its own talents."

- Eric Hoffer

My Dearest...

In the context of this book, let us start with a prelude to THOUGHT. Everything begins with a thought. So, it is said that 'Even before the seed of ***THOUGHT*** is sown by us, there is a desire or an intention.' Desires are the earliest precursor to thoughts and intentions. Desires appear to manifest themselves from the depths of the human spirit, from a deeply unique place, shaped by perspectives that can sometimes befuddle one's own cognitive reality. It is easy, and even fallacious, to conclude that desires are entirely a product of the human spirit's volition. However, desires could also have components that are derived from innate human nature, that are not always shaped by an individual's external reality. Desires eventually take root as thought, which then leads to intention and sometimes action.

Are Desires and Intention the same?

No. They are not. Desire is a state of feeling- in the realm of one's imagination, while Intention strengthens the desire with commitment to achieve the same, with an expected outcome, manifested in the physical.

Write down all your desires in these areas of your life.

Physical:

____

____

Financial:

____

____

Emotional:

____

____

Spiritual:

____

____

Social:

____

____

Can we choose our intention?

Yes. With careful and conscious practice and self-awareness, we can choose our intention and NOT be swayed by our individual life circumstances, to lead a fated existence.

Desire has to do with a wish or a longing for something, someone, or for a particular experience. We experience this in the realm of thought.

Intention has to do with a purpose, upon which one's mind is concentrated and fixed. Intention comes from the Latin "Intendere" which means to lean towards, to move towards. This is the source of the energy that moves us in the desired direction.

Learn to harness the power of intention, and you can create anything you desire.

The key thing to meditate upon and understand here is that you can direct your life's destiny through the attainment of life-transforming desires.

BHAG – Big Hairy Audacious Goal.

What is your BHAG? What do you aspire for?

1

____

____

____

2

____

____

____

3

____

____

____

Desires and Intentions can be positive or negative. How can they be negative? Wishing ill-will to someone, jealousy, hatred and other self-abusing emotions are also intentions. But let us look at a positive intention or desire. Wanting to improve your local community through service (such as literacy or self-employment), to become an actor, teach, drive a car, dance, run a marathon. It's your dream, your desire and consequently your intention, that you set in motion.

We are a bundle of our choices and contradictions, shaped by our past experiences, external inputs, internalizing it in the language we understand and painting our intentions with the brush of doubt or hope. Age, experience, ability to overcome our fears, and personal beliefs influence our intention. We can practice creating intention of the highest vibration. The power of choice is ours. It is our choices and not our abilities that make us who we are. Desire/Intention builds a strong thought process in us.

An intention is like a mantra that you keep wishing silently, till you are willing to manifest it to the world outside.

———————————

"Attention energizes, Intention transforms"

– Deepak Chopra

———————————

"Desire is possibility seeking expression."

– Ralph Waldo Emerson

———————————

"Human Behaviour flows from three main sources: Desire, Emotion and Knowledge."

– Plato

———————————

"The significance of a man is not in what he attains, but rather what he longs to attain."

– Khalil Gibran

———————————

What do you intend to do with your intention? When you act upon your intention, it will create your destiny. Have the right intentions for your life and create your destined lifestyle. It is all in your hands.

The indispensable first step to getting the things you want out of life is this: **Decide what you want**.

Know yourself.
Setting goals help us reach our aspirations.

Write down your goals and look at them to keep them in mind.

Practice setting small, doable goals, which will motivate you to build yourself.

Where your destiny is concerned, you need to set actionable goals for each phase. Break them into small parts.

With the big picture in mind (Destiny), start creating your goals.

So, set goals for the various aspects of your life — mental, health, emotional, financial, career, family, relationships, social, spiritual, etc.

List your Hobbies:

____

____

____

List your Strengths:

____

____

____

List your Areas of Improvement:

____

____

____

Ask yourself these questions

What are the milestones along the way that will let you know you are on the right track? It is crucial that we recognize those moments of intermediate achievements. "Inches make champions," said American legendary football coach, Vince Lombardi.

When you understand yourself, you will understand your challenges too. Challenges help us grow. Do not run away from them. Work on the challenges, the mental blocks. Take support. Read. Have a mentor. Attend workshops and trainings. Be updated.

Build up on your Resources - Attitude, Skills, Knowledge, People, Beliefs.

What is the outcome that you want? Start from there. How important is achieving your goal for you. How willing are you to change yourself?

What is the higher purpose?

What is the first step that you will be taking to achieve your goal?

FOOD FOR THOUGHT

There is a school of thought which feels that we should let go of all our desires if we want liberation, if we do not want to face any disappointments. But isn't wanting liberation or moksha or enlightenment, in itself a desire? *(Thinking aloud here)*

What are the areas that need your attention and focus on personal development?

Above all, it is also important to maintain a level of behavioural flexibility rather than rigidity, allowing for a series of tests, feedback and adjustments, in order to increase the level of success towards a sustainable outcome.

Having meditated and acted upon the above, you can easily realize how powerful are your naturally occurring and often instinctual desires and intentions, and how with understanding the insights and implementing the actions recommended in the following chapters can lead you to manifest your destiny!

So, my dear........................... Begin today. Write down your deepest desires and intentions and how you are going to shape your thoughts.

THATHASTHU!   SO BE IT!   AMEN!

With Immense Love,

Kalyani

2

On THOUGHTS!

(THOUGHTS LEAD TO DESTINY)

"In the egoic state, your sense of self, your identity, is derived from your thinking mind - in other words, what your mind tells you about yourself: the storyline of you, the memories, the expectations, all the thoughts that go through your head continuously and the emotions that reflect those thoughts. All those things make up your sense of self."

Eckhart Tolle

Imagine a magic genie comes to you and says that your wish, your desire is its command. Ask any three. What will you ask?

1.____

____

____

____

2.____

____

____

____

3.____

____

____

____

My Dearest ....,

The other day you were asking me as to how you can achieve your dreams and create your own destiny. Let me share with you these six proven universal laws to help you along the way with their aides.

The first step is self-awareness. '***Know Thyself***' is the greatest two-word philosophy ever written in mankind. Understanding what you want and why you want it, creates a blueprint for all the other processes.

And the first Law is **THOUGHTS**. What are thoughts? Where do they come from? Do they come from outside or within? How does it affect our destiny? Can we really create our destiny?

Thoughts are **mental cognitions — our ideas, opinions, and beliefs about ourselves and the world around us**. They include the perspectives we bring to any situation or experience that color our point of view (for better, worse, or neutral). Where do thoughts originate from? Even if there are external influences, thoughts originate from within us. They originate from our brain (mind) but takes life in our hearts (emotions).

____

"We cannot solve our problems with the same thinking we used when we created them."

Albert Einstein

____

"Whatever we think about and thank about, we bring about."

____

"The mind is everything. What you think, you become."

Buddha

____

"You don't have to learn how to control your thoughts; you just have to stop letting them control you."

____

Everything begins with a thought. Thought is the first seed that you plant to create your destiny. There was a little boy who planted a seed, dug it out every day, replanted it, watered it and observed the growth. What do you think happened? The plant did not grow at all. Dejected, the little boy runs to his mother for answers. And she told him very patiently that after planting a seed, you must water it and take care of it from external obstacles to its growth but trust in the process that it will grow.

Likewise, your thought is a seed. Once planted, work towards its growth, take care of it, nurture it, do not keep doubting yourself and go back to where you began. Hold on to it. Now, give energy to that thought. Protect it from external negativity and internal doubts. If a thought has come to you, there is every probability that it is going to happen. The Universe is working with you to make your dreams come true. It is your partner in happiness.

Thoughts have a life of their own. They breathe emotion. They vibrate. They impact you in every way. Physically, Mentally and Emotionally.

List down your fears that is preventing you from creating your own reality:

____

____

____

____

____

____

____

____

Thoughts are powerful. Remember, you **OWN** your thoughts. You can replace every undesirable thought with a positive one. This calls for conscious action, a deliberate choice - to choose what you think. So, a thought is something that you can create, feel, destroy, replace, and build on.

THINK OF WHAT YOU WANT, NOT WHAT YOU FEAR – This is one of the most favourite lifelines I use for myself. It is from the book SAM - The Magic genie by Brian Mayne. Most times, we think of what we don't want. For example, if you want to excel in your exams, or start your own business, we often think of 'What-ifs'(What if I fail) or fear of failure. Instead, practice thinking of what you want. And that brings a paradigm shift in our mind-set and thought patterns.

You would have heard so many people say that what they prayed or wished should not happen, has happened. And then we blame God, the Universe and others. Why are we even praying or thinking about what shouldn't happen?

The Cognitive Triangle

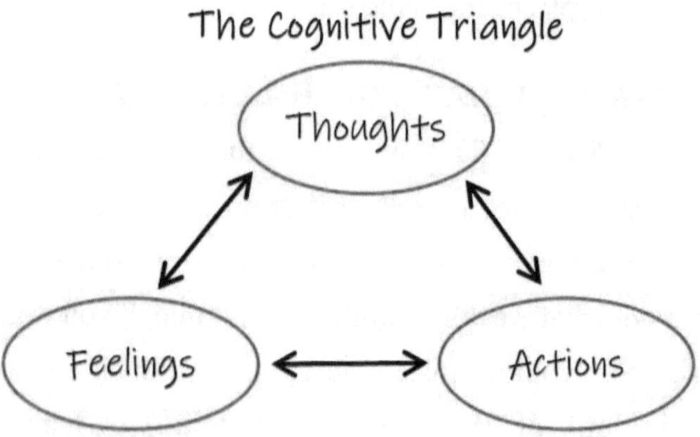

So, replace your fear thought with your want thought - your happy, magic thought. Look within. Observe your thoughts. This is the beginning of your road map to your Destiny. Thoughts are so powerful, that whatever we think, we can conjure it. The magic thus is in our hands.

"I Think. Therefore, I am." – **Rene Descartes**

Do Thoughts have life on its own? No. We give them life by breathing in our intent and emotions. Every thought that we think, develops into a bigger self and what we give most energy to, starts growing. Happy, positive thoughts keep growing happier and sad thoughts – sadder.

Imagine that every thought that you hold and give energy to, has life and takes shape and grows in proportion to the attention we give our thought. So, observe the attention you give to a thought. The time and energy you put on a thought. It is directly proportional to the outcome of your thought.

I know what is on your mind now. This is a general outlook on thoughts, but how is it affecting your destiny? Right?

Write down your five most important aspirations/goals:

____

____

____

____

____

____

____

____

____

SO, now I want you to write down five of your most important aspirations, the dreams that you have around that. Every aspiration is a seed, a thought which was planted in your brain, in your heart.

THOUGHTS AND INTENT

Thoughts in the mind, affects our body. It is all interrelated. For example, if you are sad and feel like a failure, remember, you are thinking you are a failure, you feel you are a failure and start behaving so. You will automatically carry all the body language of an unhappy, miserable person -slumped shoulders, stooping, nervous and fidgety, unable to smile and more.

Do you remember when granny was sick for some time, and doctors couldn't diagnose the reason, and they said it is psychosomatic?

Well, you must know that our thoughts affect not only our mind, but also our body. So, isn't it important to understand our thoughts?

This secret revolves around this simple idea: *You are what you think.*

SPEED OF THOUGHT

While light travels at the rate of 186,000 miles per second, thoughts virtually travel in no time. Thought is finer than ether, the medium of electricity. **Thoughts excel light in speed**. It takes 500 milliseconds, or half a second, for sensory information from the outside world to be incorporated into conscious experience.

Do you know how many thoughts we think per day? Well, a normal healthy brain has 60,000-70,000 thoughts per day. Woah! and out of that, close to 70% is negative thoughts? Now, isn't that food for thought? 

Do you know that THOUGHTS have a pattern, that we create? Complicated or simple, we are masters at it. As we repeat thought patterns, they become subconscious behavioral patterns that drive our life.

So how do you change your reality?

You create new patterns that create a new reality.

You recondition yourself.

This isn't something that happens overnight, this is a lifetime commitment to mindful reprogramming and growth. It's what neuroscientists refer to as neuroplasticity — the idea that you can rewire your brain by creating new behavioral patterns where new cells fire together and wire together.

And in order to do this, you need to understand that you are not your thoughts, you are the thoughts you give power and attention to — you are the thinker. Your thoughts are endless ideas and feelings in your mind and they are powerless until you decide to cling onto one of them. This very act makes you **the thinker** of your thoughts.

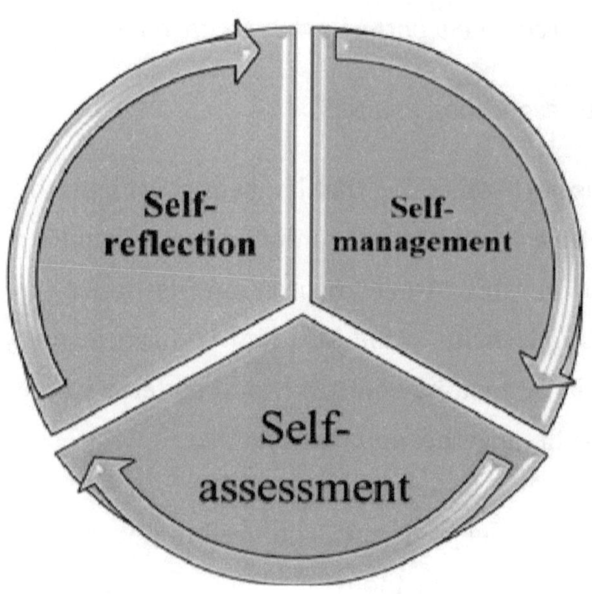

Self-reflection
Self-management
Self-assessment

In other words, imagine your mind to be a farm and your thoughts to be the seeds. You can sow either good seeds (roses) or bad seeds (poison ivy). Whichever seed you choose to focus on and sow, it will then grow and multiply. And the same happens in your mind —whichever thought you choose to focus on and sow, it will then grow into a plant and multiply.

You are the Sower of the seeds.

You are the thinker of your thoughts.

How do you create new behavioural patterns? You create new thought patterns.

And how do you create new thought patterns?

Here's how:

1. Increase your awareness by observing your emotions and body reactions.

2. Be more conscious of what thoughts you give your attention to.

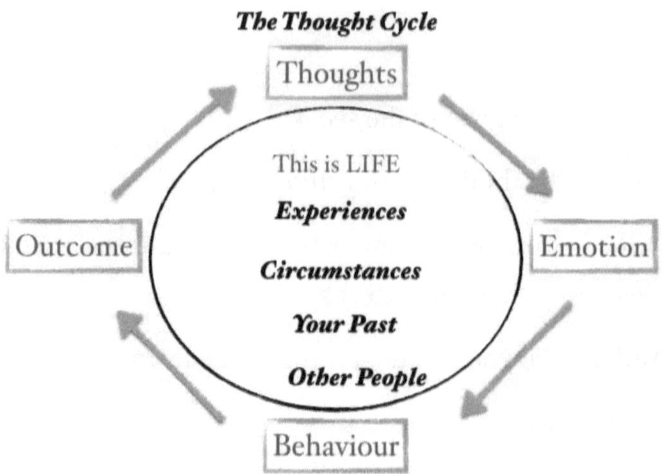

The Thought Cycle
Thoughts
This is LIFE
Experiences
Circumstances
Your Past
Other People
Outcome
Emotion
Behaviour

You cannot achieve greatness with a small mind. You have to first think big, beyond yourself. To achieve excellence, you do not need more degrees, better skills or enhanced connections. All you need is improved thoughts!

Take charge of your Mindset and Control your thoughts. Identify the thoughts you want to change.

This can help us figure out why we're feeling what we're feeling and drive us back to the root cause of these feelings: the thoughts we first gave our attention to.

As author and master trainer of Neurolinguistic Programming Michael Neill explains:

> *"It's not the thoughts that pass through your head that impact your life; it's the one you take possession of and think about all day long. Once we agree to give our attention to a thought, it becomes more and more real to us over time and has more and more power over our life."*

(Adapted from Lovett, 2008)

Thoughts are the harbinger of goals.

A thought to do something is the birth of a goal. To have clarity in thought, ask yourself these questions.

You wrote your BHAG and other desires. Now, decide how you are going to act on it and measure the progress. Which goal are you giving more attention to? Create a planner, spreadsheets, accountability partner and a routine to see through your goal. Be as specific as possible. SPECIFIC IS TERRIFIC.

1. What is the timeframe for you to achieve this goal? For things that need to happen soon or short- term goals, have a 90- day timeframe. For larger goals, which may take some years, map out sub-goals to reach there.

2. Take your goal statement and list the specific things you are already actively doing, or have you already achieved, to help to reach your goal.

3. Based on your timeframe for the overall goal, what is the specific time frame for each of these steps?

Ways to improve your physical health:

____

____

____

What bad habits do you want to change?

____

____

____

What relationship patterns do you want to improve?

____

____

____

What skills do you want to learn?

____

____

____

Remember the popular acronym S.M.A.R.T. for goals.

S – Specific

M – Measurable

A – Achievable

R – Realistic

T - Timely

What you want to achieve as goals are first in your thoughts. Put them to paper. It will give you clarity. Clarity of purpose is important for you to start putting your thoughts to action.

Write every thought- goal down. Then break them down into why you want to do, how you are going to do and by when. Prioritize.

A thought triggers an emotion. And Emotions give life to our thoughts which then triggers a body reaction and drives us to act in a certain way. This thought pattern creates a mental circuit in our brain, and as we repeat it, it becomes a subconscious behavioral pattern that runs on automation. This is how your thoughts shape your reality. Therefore, you are what you think.

"It is the quality of our thoughts, then, that create the quality of our life.

If you get the inside right, the outside will fall into place."

*- **Eckhart Tolle***

"As a man thinks, so he is; as he continues to think, so he remains."

*- **James Allen***

"A man's life is what his thoughts make of it."

- Roman emperor **Marcus Aurelius**

"A man is what he thinks about all day long."

- **Ralph Waldo Emerson**

"We become what we think about,"

- Author **Earl Nightingale**

"Life consists mainly of the storm of thoughts that is forever flowing through one's head."

*- **Mark Twain***

The next time you feel a strong emotion, bring your awareness to it by pausing and asking yourself:

What's going on in my mind right now?

Why am I feeling this way?"

Why am I happy?

Why am I feeling so low?

Why am I hopeful?

Thoughts and emotions have to be aligned. You cannot think something and feel differently. Our thoughts take us captive, though we are the ones creating our thoughts.

And this is why all the great minds and thinkers agree that we live in a world of thought. Our thoughts create our experiences, and thus, we experience what we think. The quality of our thoughts creates the quality of our life. Take a few moments and think deeply about your life. Identify where you really need to change to help you create your own destiny.

VISION BOARD

Create a vision board. Collect pictures and words around your goals and stick them on the board.

Have an ideal dream relationship with your family?

Have your own business?

Want to be healthy and happy – live a disease-free life?

Want to Travel around the world?

Want to sleep peacefully?

For example, if you want to own a yacht and travel the world, find a picture of a yacht, and paste it in the vision board.

A healthier you? go ahead, paste one of your best pics.

A mansion by the beach? It's yours - if you truly believe it and work for it.

Complete the vision board – Use bold colorful pictures and words. Put up your picture too. Vision Boards work effectively on our subconscious minds.

Take a new notebook or diary. Or use the Creating my Destiny page on your left to start with. Sit down in a quiet place, comfortably, relax yourself and gather all your thoughts. Breathe – in and out. Observe your breath. This helps in gathering our strayed thoughts.

The quality of our thoughts creates the quality of our life. Take a few moments and think deeply about your life. Identify where you really need to change to help you create your own destiny.

Before you go on to the next chapter, which is on Emotions, I am going to give you a few exercises and share some tools for you to practice and implement.

The personal tools for thought awareness

- Mindful Meditation

- Self -control

- Guided Imagery /Positive thinking

- Vision Board

CREATING MY DESTINY

Now, jot down all the thoughts – around your aspirations. Silly or profound, is not for you to decide. Write them down- happily.

Now align your thoughts with your hobbies and strengths. (A CHART on the left page)

THATHASTHU!   SO BE IT!   AMEN!

With Immense Love,

Kalyani

3

EMOTIONS

(Thoughts in motion)

"EMOTIONS *can*

GET IN THE WAY

or

GET YOU ON YOUR WAY."

My Dearest ……………………………,

Trust you had time to read and reflect on my mail to you. I am so happy you asked me this question about creating our own destiny. As I share with you my thoughts on this beautiful subject, I hope it helps you and others who read it, when you share with them.

 Like our Thatha (Grandfather in Tamil) always says, 'We need to make time for what is important for us.' Prioritize what we do. If you want to create your own destiny, one of the laws of the Universe, is to prioritize your actions and choose what you want to do. I call it the Law of Free Will.

In my previous letter to you, I had mentioned that thoughts become alive and takes shape, in proportion to the attention we give to it. The more we focus on our thoughts and add our emotions to it, a thought becomes stronger and takes deep root in our conscious mind. A very thought of an incident in our life can trigger happiness, sadness, anger, disgust, fear or anticipation. It is because of the emotion we attach with that incident.

An incident or experience remains in our conscious and sub-conscious mind, stays there quietly. Depending on the importance we attach to it, it becomes a memory which we can recall as a thought in a millisecond.

Thoughts have no value without emotion. And in this book, thoughts mean – intention, desire, dream, aspiration or goals.

"Emotions," wrote **Aristotle** (384–322 BCE), "are all those feelings that so change men as to affect their judgements, and that are also attended by **pain** or pleasure. Such are **anger**, pity, fear and the like, with their opposites. Some emotions are short-lived and instantaneous, like embarrassment or a sudden burst of anger. While some are long-lived. Such as simmering resentment, love. This translates to a facial expression or body language. Emotions leave an imprint and a lasting impact on our conscious and sub-conscious minds. We are driven by emotions. We are creatures with emotion.

Emotions shape our character.

All of us have emotions. Some of us exhibit it openly while others don't. We see that in our own family. Your aunt V is like that. Open about her thoughts, feelings and emotions. Speaks rapidly, shares her view -right or wrong. I can imagine your grin when you recall all those moments with her. ☺ And, she says she is emotionally strong. Well, there are so may terms added to the word emotion, nowadays. Emotionally strong, weak, emotional- intelligence, emotional -quotient, emotional balance and more. It doesn't matter. To each its own. That's all. But hey, I am digressing here. The only reason, I bought up the topic of emotion – is its influence on thoughts.

The 90-second chemical reaction of emotions

The theory of constructed emotion explains how emotions happen and are built up. We humans construct our emotions based on two things:
- our physiological experience of a situation, and
- our personal interpretation of it.

This also gives us the power to manage and control our emotions.

Dr. **Jill Bolte Taylor**, Harvard brain scientist explains:

> *"When a person has a reaction to something in their environment, there's a 90 second chemical process that happens in the body; after that, any remaining emotional response is just the person choosing to stay in that emotional loop."*

Our emotional triggers or red flags activate chemical changes within our body which puts us on full alert: the ***fight, flight, or freeze*** response. For these chemicals to be totally flushed out of our body it takes less than 90 seconds. This 90 second window means you can recognize your red flags, feel the physiological changes in your body, and observe as chemicals build or fade.

After 90 seconds, the initial chemical reaction is over. If you still feel fear, anger, anxiety, or any other emotion, it's not your physiology that's fueling it – it's your own thoughts re-stimulating the chemical changes.

These thoughts construct a feedback loop which re-activate the chemical response and embed the emotion deeper. So, you could say that our uniquely human ability to think makes it possible for us to get stuck in the emotional loop. This 90 second window places responsibility for emotional self-awareness and regulation on us and aligns with the theory of constructed emotion.

Let us talk on ***Emotional Empowerment*** where you take charge of your emotions. You may be conscious of your emotion- wallowing in it or it may pass by you unconsciously. We go through a range of emotions at different points in our lives with different people. Suppressed emotion will manifest itself sometime. Age, experience, circumstances and people and our own self-introspection, impacts our emotions.

When we aspire to do something in our life, how does emotion play a role? Like we can choose our thoughts, we can choose our emotions too.

Emotion is like watering the seed of thought -gently. Give it the right emotion. Feel it. Feel the aspiration. Start visualizing how it is going to be when you achieve that. Visualize yourself creating your own path – to reach your destiny.

Of course, there will be struggles and obstacles. Look at the challenges as a learning curve and prod ahead.

Your Emotion has to have a vibration - which will then tune in with the frequency of the Universe.

Are you vibrating what you want?

Are your thoughts in sync with your emotions?

Become aware of what you want and what you are thinking. Is there a match?

Catch all your thoughts and emotions attached to it. And the self-talk that you are saying to yourself.

A typical example – You want to get up early every day and do some exercise before you start your day at work. (I can hear you groan!) You know that it is one of the key things when it comes to self-love – caring for oneself. But what is your inner dialogue – to yourself.

"I hate waking up early", I hardly see the sun rising and anyways why can't the sun rise late?' I am not a morning person'. I hate mornings -so on and so forth. When there is a big gap between, what we think and what we want – you land up saying what you think. The words then reflect on your mindset and attitude – about which we shall see more in chapter III. And do you know that one of the reasons for stress is when the gap between what we do and what we want to do is wide. Wider the gap, bigger the stress.

Basically, dear ...., your thoughts and emotions and words must align with what you want.

Thoughts <----> Emotions <----> Words

How you think and how you feel directly impact how your body reacts, and all three influence how you behave and what actions you take.

"Emotion is created by Motion. Whatever you are feeling right now is related to how you are using your body"

Have you observed this? While asking people, 'HOW ARE YOU'? what does it mean? It is actually, how are you feeling? or how are you doing? It is not 'how are you thinking?'

Even before we consciously think and say something, we feel it. If X says, "I am feeling tired", he is not thinking he should feel tired.

He is just voicing out his feeling/ emotion of his current state of mind/body - which he vocalizes as words – aloud or to himself and this in turn becomes a stronger thought.

The first aspect is FEELING. When he gives energy to this thought, the tiredness worsens, and his body behaves the way he feels and thinks. This does not mean his tiredness does not exist. Once he feels this, he should take constructive steps to make himself feel better, observe if this is a pattern or take rest and mentally and emotionally decide to take actionable steps to feel better. No one wants to be unhealthy and tired all the time unless you want self-pity and misery gives you a sense of entitlement and importance and a warped sense of joy.

The second aspect to our emotions on thoughts is the unconscious way we visualize in our mind. However, when we attach an emotion to the visual picture we have in our minds, it immediately reflects in our body and mind. Emotions affect our perception, learning, memory, reasoning, and attention. It affects our behavior.

The emotions you feel each day can compel you to take action and influence the decisions you make about your life, both large and small.

Emotions are energy, moving through our body. According to a study the emotional brain is considered to have executive power in the brain. It influences all decision making, thought processes, memories, and present experiences.

How can Emotions help you reach your goal and create your own destiny?
- Makes you feel connected to your goal
- Empowers
- Create a Balance
- Help in right decision making

"Everything you do is triggered by an emotion of either desire or fear."

Brian Tracy

"Unexpressed emotions will never die. They are buried alive and will come forth later in uglier ways."

Sigmund Freud

"Emotional awareness means what you are feeling and why."

Sigmund Freud

- Help you fight for what you want (Not Freeze or Flee when there is an obstacle)
- Help you succeed.

Remember, the emotions that accompany your desires and actions, will directly influence how your dreams manifest your destiny!

THATHASTHU!   SO BE IT!   AMEN!

With Immense Love,

Kalyani

4

WORDS...WORDS...WORDS...

Words Create Worlds

"Words can Inspire.

And words can Destroy.

Choose yours well."

My Dearest------------------------------,

Thank you so much for your sweet letter and the kind words. Felt on top of the world. Your words make me feel that I am doing the right thing by sharing my thoughts with you. And if you and your friends find it useful, it makes me happy. My emotion 😊

You know that whatever I am writing here comes from the bottom of my heart and with immense love. I want you to achieve your dreams and create your own destiny. You can and you will.

Like thoughts and emotions spring from within us, so do words. We think words are audible when we speak with others. But what about the inner dialogue-words we tell ourselves, every day?

Dear ...., this is something I so believe in – the POWER OF WORDS. This is the second law.

Since the beginning of language and communication, words have got their own power.

Do you know, our ancient scriptures say that we are surrounded by spirits and angels. Whatever we say or think deeply, the spirits say ' THATHASTHU' – which means SO BE IT !

The word Asthu means WORD. Thatha + Asthu means whatever u say, let it happen, SO BE IT! Whether it is negative or positive, and you will be surprised to know that the word AMEN also means the same. SO is the case with Amin, Inshallah.....................................

This powerful philosophy is part of every religion.

'In the beginning was the Word, and the Word was with God, and the Word was God.' These are among the most famous lines in the New Testament Bible. they begin the Gospel of St. John. Come to think! This Biblical verse is so profound on the impact of tangible words. Words actually manifest our thoughts.

Recall the time when there was a function in our house and granny was saying aloud and praying that nothing negative should happen and spoil the function? Right thoughts actually. Yet....

Unfortunately, the neighbour, opposite our house passed away suddenly and we had a muted function. The celebration was low key. Now, nothing wrong in what she wished. Her desire was that there should be enjoyment, celebration, and everyone should be happy, and the function has to go the way she had envisaged. But she was instead voicing out her fears. And fears have the highest energy. All our fears come true. Because, our thoughts, our words and our body language emit fear. And that is the message you are passing on to the Universe.

List down your fears that stop you from doing what you want to do:

____

____

____

____

____

____

____

____

____

The scent of fear is heavy and attracts more energy – wild animals in the African savannah catch this instinctly, and we humans also have fear. Fear of the unknown. Fear does not mean caution. Fear is something which cripples you.

So, instead of thinking of what we don't want to happen, instead of thinking of what we fear, practice thinking and feeling and voicing WHAT YOU WANT, NOT WHAT YOU FEAR OR DON'T WANT.

I know it is easier said than done. But trust me, rather trust in yourself - all it needs is conscious practice and observing the way we think and act upon and the emotions we feel.

> "If we understood the power of our thoughts, we would guard them more closely. If we understood the awesome power of our words, we would prefer silence to almost anything negative. In our thoughts and words, we create our own weaknesses and our own strengths. Our limitations and joys begin in our hearts. We can always replace negative with positive."
>
> -Betty Eadie

Empowering words you need to tell yourself everyday with absolute belief– Aloud and in silence. List them here. It has to align with your thoughts and aspiration and end goal.

____

____

____

____

____

____

____

____

____

____

Words have a vibration. Every syllable we utter has an energy. Because every word is full of emotion. We enact the words through our body language. The intent is there in the words we utter.

So, catch your thoughts. Observe them. Are they in alignment with what you want? What are the words that are coming out from your mouth? If your thoughts, words and emotion is not in alignment with what you want- CHANGE THE THOUGHT. It is possible, because remember, you own your thoughts.

A poster on a school notice board declares: "What we habitually say in our heads, we usually end up saying in our lips, which ultimately directs our feet"

I do agree, not everything can go as we plan. In those instances, it is important for us to learn the lessons that the universe is teaching us, through the incident.

There will be obstacles, challenges and trials and tribulations. How we manage ourselves and handle the challenge is what will take us one step closer to our destined future.

Daily Affirmations

Print the affirmations and tape it where you will read it more often. You can print it in more than one place. The affirmations should get into your subconscious mind. You could also try mirror affirmations.

I am a blessed soul.

I am beautiful and I love myself

I am receiving the best guidance from the Universe.

I am blessed with abundance in health, thoughts, emotions and wealth.

I am grateful for all the experiences and events in my life and for the people who have touched my life

I forgive myself.

I attract what I seek.

I am the creator of my own destiny.

I love these words which I read on a website. **Words have energy and power with the ability to help, to heal, to hinder, to hurt, to harm, to humiliate and to humble**. Words create actions and reactions.

We all need to harness the power of words for our self - transformation. This book will not be complete without this chapter. Because it is from here – that we create our path to Destiny.

How do we do that? Let me share an incident with you. Do you recall what your younger brother used to say very often? That he would start his own business and give employment to many people. Though our family was not very encouraging about it, nor did they take him seriously, from the age of 14, he used to keep saying this. He went on to complete his post-graduation and started working. We all assumed he had forgotten about his desire for acting. But when he was 24 and a few months after his birthday, he started his own organization and has employed around 30 people. Good for a start-up. That is the Power of words. The Universe answered his desire.

SERENITY PRAYER

God, grant me the serenity

To accept the things I cannot change,

The courage to change the things I can,

And the wisdom to know the difference.

(Attributed to Reinhold Niebuhr, Lutheran theologian)
(1892–1971)

How the Words We Choose Shape Our Lives?

Their power arises from our emotional responses when we read, speak, or hear them. For example, just say the word 'Snake' while in a party, or in the workplace, or in a crowded theatre, and you'll get three completely different but powerful emotional and energetic reactions. Even the words of others can easily affect our personal vibration. Spend a few minutes with a cribber, complaining all the time, and using negative terms, you'll feel your personal energy bottom out. Words have great power, so choose them (and your friends) wisely!

Yes. The Universe is listening to all our words and intentions and desires. Like Paulo Coelho says in his book ALCHEMIST – when you want something very badly, the entire Universe conspires in its favor. So, do you want to achieve something? and desire deeply for that to happen? Then, think about it, add intention and emotion to that desire, vocalize it, say it aloud, start believing in it, and START WORKING TOWARDS IT. You have to prepare for it too.

"There is power in words. What you say is what you get."

- Zig Ziglar

"Raise your words, not your voice. It is rain that grows flowers, not thunder."

-Rumi

"Handle them carefully, for words have more power than atom bombs."

-Pearl Strachan Hurd

"Throughout human history, our greatest leaders and thinkers have used the power of words to transform our emotions, to enlist us in their causes, and to shape the course of destiny. Words cannot only create emotions, they create actions. And from our actions flow the results of our lives."

- Tony Robbins

"Be careful what you say. You can say something hurtful in ten seconds, but ten years later, the wounds are still there."

- Joel Osteen

"Words have energy and power with the ability to help, to heal, to hinder, to hurt, to harm, to humiliate, and to humble."

- Yehuda Berg

Because, when what you want comes to you, you need to be in a position to receive it. You must be ready for it. What you say to yourself has more power than what others say to you.

Words can transform the entire world. Great leaders and speakers rely on the spoken word. Oral or written, words have POWER.

Do not be casual about words. Don't throw away words carelessly. Words that you wouldn't mean. We say things like, "I hate my hair," "I'm so stupid," "I'm such a useless person." We never think that these words bring negative energy into our vibration and affect us on a physical level, but they do. Emoto's experiments were conducted with water. Why? Because sound vibration travels through water four times faster than it does through open air. Our body is over 70% water, and you'll understand how quickly the vibration from negative words resonates in your cells. Ancient scriptures tell us that life and death are in the power of the tongue.

Water and Words

Japanese scientist, Masaru Emoto performed some of the most fascinating experiments on the effect that words have on energy in the 1990's. When frozen, water that's free from all impurities will form beautiful ice crystals that look exactly like snowflakes under a microscope. Water that's polluted, or has additives like fluoride, will freeze without forming crystals.

In his experiments, Emoto poured pure water into vials labeled with negative phrases like "I HATE YOU" or "FEAR." After 24 hours, the water was frozen, and no longer crystallized under the microscope: It yielded gray, misshapen clumps instead of beautiful lace-like crystals. In contrast, Emoto placed labels that said things like "I LOVE YOU," or "PEACE" on vials of polluted water, and after 24 hours, they produced gleaming, perfectly hexagonal crystals.

Some of us are in the habit of using the same negative words over and over again out of habit. The problem is that the more we hear, read, or speak a word or phrase, the more power it has over us.

This is because the brain uses repetition to learn, searching for patterns and consistency as a way to make sense of the world around us. Only after being burned a few times can we understand that fire is always hot.

Speak to yourself like someone you love. Encourage yourself, motivate yourself, and uplift yourself with your words.

Remember, words have a way of coming to life (often unexpectedly), influencing our attitudes, actions, habits and eventually our character. Irrespective of how we perceive their effect, our words eventually impact how effectually our dreams realize their manifest destiny.

Therefore, it is our responsibility to choose the right words, set the right intent and course of actions, to manifest what we want!

Water and Words *Contd...*

Emoto's experiments proved that energy generated by positive or negative words can actually change the physical structure of an object. The results of his experiments were detailed in a series of books beginning with THE HIDDEN MESSAGES IN WATER, where you can see the astounding before and after photos of these incredible water crystals.

In another experiment, Emoto tested the power of spoken words. He placed two cups of cooked white rice in two separate mason jars and fixed the lids in place, labelling one jar "THANK YOU" and the other, "YOU FOOL." The jars were left in an elementary school classroom, and the students were instructed to speak the words on the labels to the corresponding jars twice a day. After 30 days, the rice in the jar that was constantly insulted had shrivelled into a black, gelatinous mass. The rice in the jar that was thanked was as white and fluffy as the day it was made. This dramatic example of the power of words is also detailed in Emoto's book.

How can Right Words Accelerate your Goals

- Brings Positive vibration and clarity

- Creates an energy and supports your desire

- Writing your goals down and saying affirmations, actualises it

- Words have power and Life and helps you in your action.

- Words are a great way to express what we want.

- Words uplift you to act. The more you say something to yourself, you start believing in it.

In our journey towards manifesting our dreams to destiny, words play a great role in giving life to manifestation.

My dearest ...., Speak wise words and manifest what you Desire!

THATHASTHU!   SO BE IT!   AMEN!

With Immense Love,

Kalyani

5

MANIFESTATION

(Ask and it shall be given;
Seek and ye shall find;
Knock and it shall be opened)

"What you think you become. What you feel you attract. What you imagine you create."

—Buddha

"To bring anything into your life, imagine that it's already there."

Richard Bach

My Dearest.................................,

In our entire journey of self- awakening and creating our destiny, it is so important to learn how to manifest what we want. From thoughts – words, every step, we are creating an inner field and attracting what we want.

What is Manifestation? Manifestation is based on the Universal Principle of Law of Attraction. It is the magic key given to each of us by the Universe.

Manifestation is **to create something or turn something from an idea into a reality**. In psychology, manifestation generally means using our *thoughts, feelings, and beliefs* to bring something to our physical reality. We live the reality of the future, in our present state and train our mind to believe that we have already achieved our goal. We experience the happiness, the success, the joy and the impact that we would have when our dream is achieved, in the manifestation field. This is a field of unlimited possibilities. This is a field of pure potentiality. When you consciously chose to manifest your desire, that is when the magic happens.

Manifestation is the process of bringing something into being or making it a reality through deliberate thought, action, and intention.

Visualization, on the other hand, is the practice of creating mental images or pictures in your mind in order to achieve a specific goal or outcome. The key difference between the two is that manifestation involves actively taking steps to bring something into being, while visualization is more focused on creating mental pictures and using them to inspire and motivate you to take action

Anyone can manifest. While we all believe and know that there is the LAW OF ATTRACTION at work here, I will call it THE LAW OF BELIEF.

Tools for Manifestation
1. Meditation
2. Visualization
3. Gratitude

You can manifest or attract something in your life, only if you *believe* it. If you do not believe in yourself, your product or service, manifestation will be impossible.

Hence aligning what we want with what we are thinking and saying and emoting is the first step.

Manifestation is our vision for our future. Here are a few pointers to manifest.

1. Write down your desires. Make a manifestation card and read it aloud twice a day, with devotion and consistency.

2. Write down in Present Tense what you want to Manifest. Believe that your desire has been fulfilled and you are living your dream life – the one you deserve and create.

   Ex: – 100 books of SO BE IT – A magic manual to turn your Dreams to Destiny is sold 😊

3. Believe in it while writing it down (scribing) while thinking or saying it aloud and send your intentions to the Universe. See your wish as already accomplished. Have unshakeable faith.

4. Meditate. Throw the If's and buts from your vocabulary.

5. Take actions to manifest your desire. Work on it.

6. Vibrate the emotions of happiness and gratitude in your physical body and create the energy of joy around you.

7. Be consistent in your thoughts /actions/ while manifesting your desires.

8. Surround yourself with people who will help you in creating your destiny.

9. Keep your heart open and read the language of the Universe.

10. Say and feel gratitude for your desires which are manifested. (Even before it is manifested) And gratitude is possible only when we get what we want. For feeling that immense gratitude and experiencing and vibrating joy, for something that is yet to happen but has happened in your manifestation mind, it needs Faith.

"Vision gets the dreams started. Dreaming employs your God-given imagination to reinforce the vision. Both are part of something I believe is absolutely necessary to building the life of a champion, a winner, a person of high character who is consistently at the top of whatever game he or she is in".

Emmitt Smith S.

One of the most powerful tools for manifestation is visualisation. Manifestation is not possible without visual. Because the mind thinks only in pictures.

Visualization is a powerful technique and can make all your dreams come true.

The ART OF VISUALISATION will actually help you MANIFEST your desire and making it your DESTINY. Visualization is an effective way to influence your subconscious mind.

"Your nervous system cannot tell the difference between an imagined experience and a real experience. In either case it reacts automatically to information which you give to if from your forebrain. Your nervous system reacts appropriately to what you think or imagine to be true"

Maxwell Maltz, *Psycho – Cybernetics*

Practice visualization every day, every waking minute. How would you feel when you achieve your dreams? Bring that emotion, right now. Start behaving in such a way as if your dream is already fulfilled.

And start feeling gratitude from the word go, even before you have achieved it

And oh yes, remember to use the word **WHEN** instead of **IF.** The word IF is iffy – with a doubt of whether it may or may not happen. But the word WHEN means you are confident it is going to happen, only the time is not known.

Visualization is a fine art. It needs practice. It needs inner belief. It is a skill. It is one of the greatest GIFTS that humans possess. Visualization brings instant effects in your body and mind.

Do this exercise – Close your eyes and visualize your favourite biriyani that aunty S makes – visualize in pictures. Mouth -watering, isn't it?

There is no greater example for visualization than food – the very thought -with added emotion alters our mind and body. Or thinking of people we love, who are not with us.

Visioning and Envisioning are two techniques for manifesting your goals and creating your destiny.

Like Vishen Lakhani, founder of Mind Valley says,

*"**ENVISIONING** is when you imagine certain events or outcomes like video game walk-throughs so you can effortlessly turn them into reality."*

How does that differ from the visualization?

VISUALIZATION refers to creating visual aids that can accelerate learning and in turn, achieve your goals.

Here is a list of the techniques that relate to **visualization** in psychology:

1. Create pictures representing your goals and place them in prominent positions around your home or workspace.

2. Create affirmation cards and read them as many times as possible in a day, with faith.

3. Meditate. In inner silence, bring to your mind what you want and plant them in your subconscious mind. Visualize in pictures- what you want.

MEDITATION

It's one of the most powerful tools for physical, mental and emotional healing. It has been used in many different traditions and religions to help ourselves. "Meditation is the inner work of self-reflection and self-transformation through mental, physical, and emotional discipline."

- *Find a spot for yourself where you can meditate every day.*
- *Zen the place. Keep it clean and clutter free*
- *Use a yoga mat*
- *You can light a mild, aromatic incense if you feel it may help you be centered.*
- *Sit in a comfortable position in vajra asana or cross-legged.*
- *Wear comfortable clothing.*
- *Close your eyes (This aids in inner calm)*
- *Breathe gently.*
- *Observe your breath.*

In contrast, here is a list of **envisioning** techniques suggested by psychologists:

1. Meditating on certain positive thoughts, ideas, or methods to internalize them.
2. Envisioning your day in advance to avert potential threats and resolve predictable obstacles.
3. Envisioning the favorable outcome of an event to enable its occurrence.

In simple words, **the difference between vision and envisioning is within the technique**.

For visualization techniques, you need to create imagery that supports your goals, **just as Olympians do in mental training**.

As taught by Vishen, founder of Mind valley, the **envisioning method** involves meditation to look inward and create the right set of circumstances for your success. To learn more about how to create the life of your wildest dreams. The more vivid your imagination, the more effective your envisioning technique will likely be. For instance, American football coaches make their teams watch their

MEDITATION

(My suggestion on how you can start)

Option 1:

- *Release your thoughts for your destiny to the universe.*
- *Visualize the thought as if it has happened. Feel the joy.*
- *Say and feel gratitude for everything.*

(Time needed is 10 minutes. You can choose to sit longer.)

Option 2:

- *Chant the syllable OM gently. Feel its vibration. It has great impact on your body and energies.*
- *Then follow Option 1.*

There are many types of meditation, but we can begin with the easiest one.

opponents at play. This can help them visualize strategies to overcome their opponents' gameplay.

So, from the thought stage (of what you want to achieve) we have now added emotions to it and given life to our dreams. Before you proceed to the next chapter where I share with you the next process, that is –the LAW OF ACTION, in creating our destiny, do the exercises and note down your experience. This will be a great start for self-evaluation and observing the progress that you are making towards your self – discovery and creating your own destiny

At this stage, Thoughts and emotions on your aspiration is yet to be visible to the outside world. So, without any fear grow your thoughts and build strong emotions around it. Start believing in yourself. Don't hold back and restrict your thoughts and emotions on your aspirations. DARE TO DREAM! Practice Manifestation and visualization everyday.

"What lies behind you and what lies in front of you, pales in comparison to what lies inside of you."

Ralph Waldo Emerson

| **The fine art of visualization or envisioning.**

How does visualization help in manifesting your destiny?

- Picturising what you want in mind gives you clarity
- Shows you an outcome and a reality
- Creates a mental snapshot
- Gets deeper into the subconscious mind and helps you stay focussed
- Creates an energy and excitement around you
- Takes you closer to your goal

Manifestation is Magic and you are the magician here. May you start Manifesting your Dreams and create your Destiny. And start taking ACTION in the right direction.

PS: Be very careful while choosing what you want to manifest. Never try to manifest the wrong things in your life. If you wish evil for anyone, it will only affect you. Manifestation is not kind to wrong doers.

THATHASTHU!   SO BE IT!   AMEN!

With Immense Love,

Kalyani

6

ACT! ACT! ACT!

(Take massive Action)

"Act! Act! Act! Arise, stop not till the goal is reached."

— **Swami Vivekananda**

WELL DONE IS BETTER THAN WELL SAID

My Dearest...............................,

So Happy to receive your mail. And that you are sharing my mails with your friends. I am so happy to hear that your brother is starting his own venture.

My best wishes to him. I am sure he will succeed in all his endeavors if he takes the desired and necessary action.

This chapter is so apt, right now.

I was sharing with you about *the Power of Thoughts, Beliefs, Emotions and Words to help create our own Destiny*. While words have the power to manifest our reality, it is important that we get into action. Just sitting and praying without studying is not going to bring us any result. Likewise, Thoughts + Intention + Words alone cannot bring miracles. The magic is in the Action – The Third Law.

It is the easiest and the toughest. We all know that we must start doing what we want to do. Yet, we keep postponing and procrastinating. What stops us from taking action then?

"The superior man acts before he speaks, and afterwards speaks according to his actions."

– Confucius

"If you talk about it, it's a dream, if you envision it, it's possible, but if you schedule it, it's real."

– Anthony Robbins

"None of it works unless YOU work. We have to do our part. If knowing is half the battle, action is the second half of the battle."

– Anthony Robbins

Do you resonate with any of the following reasons?

- Fear of failure, of rejection, and being ridiculed.

- Lack of awareness in the area you want to start.

- Lack of planning

- Finance – inadequate funds to start with.

- Lack of awareness to use social media as a tool.

- Not prioritizing.

- Lack of time.

It could be any number of reasons, but we all know that these are nothing but excuses.

In our journey towards our destiny, the process of Thoughts and Beliefs and emotions is internal. Only we know what is happening within us. But ACTIONS SPEAK LOUDER THAN WORDS.

They bring our dreams to the physical world. It is now visible to all. The birth is over. All that remains is the christening of our desire. Now is the time to put all your ***intention into action***- step by step.

If:

A B C D E F G H I J K L M N O P Q R S T
U V W X Y Z

is represented as:

1 2 3 4 5 6 7 8 9 10 11 12 13 14 15 16 17 18 19 20
21 22 23 24 25 26

Then:

A + T + T + I + T + U + D + E

1 + 20 + 20 + 9 + 20 + 21 + 4 + 5 = **100 %**

S + K + I + L + L

19 + 11 + 9 + 12 + 12 = **63 %**

K + N + O + W + L + E + D + G + E

11 + 14 + 15 + 23 + 12 + 5 + 4 + 7 + 5 = **96 %**

Your biggest learning curve is in this process. Develop and implement all the knowledge that you need to have to fulfil your aspirations.

In our family, we always talk about the power of ASK. The Magic word I use for self-empowering and motivating myself.

A – ATTITUDE
S - SKILL
K – KNOWLEDGE

With this mantra in mind, develop the knowledge that you need. Join courses, follow leaders, get a mentor, read books. Do everything that it takes to know all about your product or service that you are planning to launch.

Then develop the SKILLS that you need for that. Communication, Marketing, Technology, Financial, Risk Appetite and all the skills required which will enhance your knowledge.

However, the most important skill you need to develop is ATTITUDE. Develop the Right Attitude. It is the key to your creating your destiny. Attitude helps you win or fail.

Three action steps that you need to take to accelerate your goal:

Attitude:

____

____

____

Skill:

____

____

____

Knowledge:

____

____

____

Attitude is Everything. Self-confidence, belief, humility, gratitude, courage. The list goes on. Attitude to change one's mindset, attitude to learn, develop habits, being persistent, knowing one's own strength and weakness. Throw away every attitude which will hinder your growth. Here, your mind set plays a huge role in creating your destiny. Saying is one thing. But doing – is real. Just like power of choice is in your hands, so is attitude.

Like Bruce Lee said, *"I fear not the man who has practiced 10,000 kicks once, but I fear the man who has practiced one kick 10,000 times."*

Practice your Attitude, your skill and keep upgrading yourself. Self-Discipline is the key word here. Nothing or no one should stop you from achieving your goal. Turn deaf to the nay sayers.

Your actions and behavior should live up to your ideals and dreams. Every action of yours should be in alignment with what you want.

Action decides your behavior. It reflects your personality, your approach towards all that you do.

List down the positive behavioral changes which will help you reach your goal:

____

____

____

____

____

____

____

____

Set Goals. Create a roadmap, an action plan to reach your destiny. However tough it gets, be prepared to change the route but not your goal. Always see how you can make things work.

Remember that "all things are created twice. Creation in the mind occurs first, then physical creation follows".

Isn't it surprising that you can always fake your words but never your actions? Your action impacts your surroundings and is the only way to create your own destiny.

An action – towards building your future is not a one-off act. It demands consistency. Consistent action any day beats talent. Consistency is an attitude, that can be developed. You just need to decide that you will never give up on what you want to do.

Consistent Actions leads to Habits – which is what we are going to discuss in our next letter.

What are the action points that you need to jot down, to create your goals? Keep them simple but decide to be consistent.

I am sharing this beautiful poem 'Psalm of Life' by H W Longfellow. Read it every day. It will be your strongest companion in times of despair and fear.

Tell me not, in mournful numbers,
Life is but an empty dream!
For the soul is dead that slumbers,
And things are not what they seem.

Life is real! Life is earnest!
And the grave is not its goal;
Dust though art, to dust returnest,
Was not spoken of the soul.

Not enjoyment, and not sorrow,
Is our destined end or way;
But to act, that each tomorrow
Find us farther than today.

Art is long, and Time is fleeting,
And our hearts, though stout and brave,
Still, like muffled drums, are beating
Funeral marches to the grave. (Contd....)

You can try creating your destiny in small areas and practice your skills, hone them and understand where are your personal pitfalls?

So, what are the steps you will now take to act upon?

Action leads to results.

Our past action has led us to what and where we are now. In the same manner, our present life will automatically create our future. It is that simple.

One needs to be very careful while choosing to act on their intent. Undoing it may cause a waste of time and money and resources. So, think through, but once you decide to act, nothing or no one should stop you. You may need to change the direction towards reaching your destiny, sometimes, but don't look back. Take actions which will help you move forward. And if you falter at one step, it is okay. Fall forward. Learn your lessons as to why you slipped and continue going.

Do not let fear be your driver in this. Fear should not paralyze you from taking actions. Be cautious yet Bold. Have the courage of conviction. And however boring or tiresome it gets, (for it will) never give up.

In the world's broad field of battle,
In the bivouac of Life,
Be not like the dumb, driven cattle!
Be a hero in the strife.

Trust no Future, howe'er pleasant!
Let the dead Past bury its dead!
Act, -- act in the living Present!
Heart within, and God o'erhead!

Lives of great men all remind us
We can make our lives sublime,
And, departing, leave behind us
Footprints on the sands of time;

Footprints, that perhaps another,
Sailing o'er life's solemn main,
A forlorn and shipwrecked brother,
Seeing shall take heart again.

Let us, then, be up and doing,
With a heart for any fate;
Still achieving, still pursuing,
Learn to labor and to wait.

How will taking right Action lead to your Destiny.

- Using the Power of Choice.
- Each Action is a step forward towards your goal.
- Your strength resolves in implementing actions towards your goal.
- A feeling of wellness and happiness, confidence and faith brings about a positive vibration and creates a sense of accomplishment.
- You start living your dream life.

Your actions have to be consistent to bring fruitful results. And develop the 'never give up' attitude.

The smallest act is grander than the greatest intention. Take MASSIVE ACTION AND YOU WILL BE BLESSED WITH MASSIVE RESULTS.

THATHASTHU!   SO BE IT!   AMEN!

With Immense Love,

Kalyani

7

IMPLEMENTATION

(Action At Work)

"It's important to have a sound idea, but the really important thing is the implementation."

— Wilbur Ross

My Dearest..

From intention to action to habits formation, we reach the most important part which will open our doors to our own Destiny. And that is *Implementation* of all that we have practiced and learnt so far.

Implementation is the act of actually making our desires happen. The act of implementation is the glue that connects the intangible, yet powerful seeds of desires, emotions and thoughts, the tangible aspects of thoughts and words, with the material aspect of action to manifest the objective of our destiny. Implementation engages the awareness and knowledge cultivated in our hearts and minds, translating our intentions into tangible actions, with a laser focus to realize our destiny. It will mean scripting every non-material desire and thought, tangible words and attitude posture, and material action in great detail. It will entail aligning our intentions, words and actions to this script, until we accomplish our desired outcome.

So, what exactly does Implementation entail? What does it take to implement the ideas presented in this book to translate your dreams and desires, into manifesting your destiny?

1. A thorough self-examination and meditation of our own self, our innate nature, our self-direction, and our aspirational values – identifying and extricating our dreams and desires from the realm of vague imagination and documenting them with intent and aspiration to manifest them.

2. Examining our thoughts, our attitudes, values and norms we hold towards our dreams and desires.

3. Examining our choice of words and dialog (internal and external) pertaining not only to our dreams and desires, but in general to our own selves, the people in our lives and our relationships, and towards our lives in general.

4. Creating a clear action plan towards manifesting our dreams and desires.

5. Mindful execution – Taking conscious actions to achieve our goals in a timely manner. Constantly reviewing progress not only in terms of steps on a spreadsheet-based tracker or mind-map, but as well on the intangible aspects such as our attitudes, thought patterns and internal/ external dialog.

6. Positive reinforcement – Frequent or daily reviews resolving to course-correct and act resolutely towards attainment, meditating to keep our emotions, attitudes, thinking and language in alignment, reading/ listening to positive books and other material that reinforce a positive mindset and winner mentality, being mindful and self-aware of distracting/ negative influences and making conscious choices to eliminate them, celebrating our everyday wins and being empathetic to our failings as fallible human beings, and finally championing our own selves as we embark on this manifestation journey.

7. Creating an Accountability framework – Treating our documentation, planning and actions towards manifesting our dreams/ desires with deep

respect, is only the first step. But how can we cultivate greater self-respect in this implementation process? Can we be part of a peer-group consisting of individuals, all manifesting their own destinies, meeting periodically to celebrate individual progress, constantly encourage and reinforce one another's journey? If not a peer-group, can we cultivate a buddy or accountability partner?

8. The birth of the new YOU is about to happen.

Implementation is specific to you, your persona and your individual life circumstances, irrespective of whether you share the same dreams as somebody else. While at the implementation stage, fine tuning is a must with the idea of reducing or eliminating imperfections in our thoughts, emotions, words and actions, it will take effort in an iterative process to perfect the same. Implementation is a combination of all our actions and habits, and it is a very critical step in bringing our desires to fruition. Presence of mind and adaptiveness is a very important skill here, in order to course correct with optimal actions in a timely manner.

An idea becomes real only if it is implemented. There is a sea change in us while we are in the process of implementing our desire. It shapes our personality and character. It defines who we are. Our Habits become seamless and implementing them in our daily life, designs our entire life/lifestyle.

The challenges we face during implementation will be real. But it is overcoming these challenges that really matters and is a test of our determination. Develop the never give up attitude. Be doggedly stubborn about getting what you want. When there are barriers, think how you can go around it. Do not give up at this stage.

The most relevant personal tool at this stage is Will Power. As the word suggests, the power to be determined is in your hands.

Steps to develop Will Power:
1. Just do it.
2. Plan and Prepare
3. Do not procrastinate.
4. Use positive affirmations
5. Learn to say no to yourself and others if something comes your way

6. Prioritise

7. Follow the 5 second rule.

8. The present and future Self has to want the same destiny. Align them.

9. Avoid Temptations.

10. Believe in yourself.

In the Implementation journey towards creating your destiny, do not start doubting yourself, when obstacles come your way. Remember, obstacles are just testing and strengthening your resolve. Rise above it.

Use your personal power of Self Reliance. Learning to rely on yourself is an important strength to have. Self-Reliance is the foundation for being independent. Self Reliance gives you confidence and courage.

Self-Reliance helps in actualizing set goals. When you are self-reliant you actually empower yourself and can independently take decisions. If you are not self-reliant and trust less in yourself, then every challenge you face will be a setback.

Learn like crazy. Be a continuous learner and keep upskilling yourself. No one can stop you. You will be unstoppable.

Take responsibility. Be accountable to yourself. No one will have the best interests of you in their hearts, more than yourself

Take control of your choices and life. You will be able to create a better balance, even in the most difficult of times.

Implementation is result and outcome focused.

Power of choice

As a thinker said, 'We cannot always choose the music life plays for us, but we can choose how we dance to it'. You are not a helpless puppet in the hands of an unknown puppeteer. Everything in life is a reflection of choices you have made in the past. To bring about a more successful and happier result, you now have to make different choices. The power lies in you to create your own destiny. With this new-found confidence, you can sculpt a brilliant future for yourself.

"Vision without implementation is counter-productive."

Douglas B. Reeves

"Inaction takes toll of your knowledge and reason too. Knowing what to do is one thing and implementing it to weed out your flaws is all together a different ball game."

Dr. Prem Jagyasi

Only you can create it—with your thoughts and deep desire and action.

One thought can change the pattern of your life. Sometimes society, nation, the whole world can transform with just a thought.

Implementation leads to tangible results which leads to your goals.

- Act Now
- Course Correct as you implement your ideas and strategies
- Keep the bigger picture in mind
- Do not give up
- Be consistent and focussed on the goal

My Dearest................................., as you implement and take continuous action, and install the necessary Habits (about which I will be sharing with you), keep visualizing and learning and taking the right actions.

THATHASTHU!   SO BE IT!   AMEN!

With Immense Love,

Kalyani

8

HABITS

The Power Vehicle to create your own Destiny

"Champions don't do extraordinary things. They do ordinary things in an extraordinary way. They do them without thinking, too fast for the other team to react. They follow the habits they've learned."

Charles Duhigg
Power of Habits

"Quality is not an act; it is a habit."

– Aristotle

My Dearest ....,

I was thrilled that you shared your POA (Plan of Action) with me. I love the consistent way you are approaching your aspirations with ambition.

Like Shakespeare says in his play Julius Caesar,

"For ambition is made of sterner stuff".

You need to be so self-aware and self-disciplined to go where you want to be.

When you take charge of your own life, you have to make personal sacrifices and compromises. No successful person had it easy in life. It is *survival of the fittest*. **The fourth law is habits.**

Habits are a set of routines that we do every day. These routines can be called as rituals too. The word ritual brings a sacredness to what we are doing. Habits become muscle memory.

Consistent Action becomes a Habit. Your brain and mind and body will get so used to the consistency, that if you don't do what you have started out to do, you will feel uncomfortable.

"First forget inspiration. Habit is more dependable. Habit will sustain you whether you're inspired or not. Habit will help you finish and polish your stories. Inspiration won't. Habit is persistence in practice."

— Octavia Butler.

"Chains of habits are too light to be felt until they are too heavy to be broken."

— Warren Buffet

The Brain is such a beautiful marvel. It can be trained. It can help you reengineer your mind set. It is a powerful tool and can be tuned to perfection with the right installation of HABITS.

How do Habits form?

First, there must be an intention to do something – an end goal -which will benefit you and give you happiness. Let us call it the REWARD – of happiness, success and achievement.

So, first see your Reward in mind. Hold it. Visualize it. You would already know how it would negatively impact you, if you do not follow what you must be doing.

The Intention(I) is the Trigger. From the place of I – you need to take action and form a relationship with TIME (T). The I and T must work together in tandem. You must also create a Warrior (W) in yourself, who will be trained to destroy any internal or external obstacle that comes in your way – to reach your goal. And yes, there will be plenty of such Obstacles. Train your warriors in your mind.

What is KAIZEN?

Kaizen is an approach to creating continuous improvement based on the idea that small ongoing positive changes can reap significant improvements.

For personal development, Kaizen is 1% improvement every day – for a thought, an action, or a habit.

Mind is a muscle. It is a great student. It just needs clear instructions. When you visualize the Reward and keep working towards it, you will start seeing results. This will keep you motivated. People are rewarded not for the attempts they make but for the results they bring.

Taste your reward. Bring your dream to Destiny. Feel it. Vibrate it in every action that you do.

Practice Kaizen in your everyday action. 1% improvement in your action- everyday. 1 % improvement in your personality building. 1 step closer to your goal. Habits are very resilient and very hard to break once made. Neuroscientists have traced our habit-making behaviours to a part of the brain called the basal ganglia, which also plays a key role in the development of emotions, memories and pattern recognition. Decisions, meanwhile, are made in a different part of the brain called the prefrontal cortex. But as soon as a behaviour becomes automatic, the decision-making part of your brain goes into a sleep mode of sorts.

"In fact, the brain starts working less and less," says Duhigg. "The brain can almost completely shut down.

List down 10 habits that are deterring you from your personal growth:

1.____

____

2.____

____

3.____

____

4.____

____

5.____

____

6.____

____

7.____

____

8.____

____

9.____

____

10.____

____

And this is a real advantage, because it means you have all of this mental activity you can devote to something else." Charles Duhigg. His new book THE POWER OF HABIT explores the science behind why we do what we do

Aristotle said: **"We are what we repeatedly do**. Excellence, then, is not an act, but a habit.

Even a genius becomes one, because he does the same thing day in and day out and excellence becomes his second nature.

Think of common examples – cycling, driving, brushing your teeth, cooking and complex things that we do every day in an automated fashion. Habits are automatic. Habits help you in managing your time effectively and aids in quick decision making.

NANO HABITS – Develop teeny-weeny nano habits. Incremental Increase brings about a huge change.

Making resolutions and deciding to form a habit is the easiest. Sustaining it is the challenge. But not impossible. There is a method to the madness.

List down 5 habits that you will follow religiously if you want to create your own destiny:

1._____________________________________

____

2._____________________________________

____

3._____________________________________

____

4._____________________________________

____

5._____________________________________

____

List down 5 habits that you should not be doing:

1._____________________________________

____

2._____________________________________

____

3._____________________________________

____

4._____________________________________

____

5._____________________________________

____

Start building NANO habits. Small habits which you will easily follow. This will build your discipline and determination too. Slow but steady n consistently.

You should focus on habit **replacement** rather than elimination. Which means, you introduce something new into your routine instead of fighting yourself to get rid of something.

As you develop a habit, drop a habit which is hindering your growth. While dropping habits, do not get into the slow and steady method. Drop it and never look back. Once again it is your mindset and determination which is put to test.

While creating new habits, we also need to understand the importance of unlearning. Some habits and mind set is so ingrained in us and so deep rooted that we find it impossible to unlearn and relearn what needs to be done.

In many cases when you unlearn something you can get rid of a bad habit, preconceptions or something that is self-sabotaging you.

Write two Life Transforming Habits /high impact habit for your personal and professional life

1.____

____

2.____

____

What influences your habits?

____

____

____

What are your triggers?

____

____

____

What motivates you?

____

____

____

Alvin Toffler, futurist and philosopher said:

"The illiterate of the 21st century will not be those who cannot read and write, but those who cannot learn, unlearn, and relearn."

Changing ourselves is vital. We need to be ready and open to change- to survive and thrive

You can do it and will do it if your desire to create your destiny is strong enough.

Do not allow negative, useless habits to take root. It all begins with a seed (action) that you sow. When you repeatedly do it, the bad habit takes root. There is no pruning it. You can only uproot the tree of Bad Habit. A bad habit is bad. No one ever says thieving, smoking or cheating is a good habit. We allow HABITS to grow on us.

Forming habits is a conscious decision and action. It is a war between what we should be doing and what we are actually doing. Again, it is a choice that we take. The power to change and implement habits is only in our hands.

The 30-Day Habits Installation Challenge

From the list of Habits that you need to install in yourself to create your destiny, identify one or two key habits and to start with and list them down:

1.____

____

2.____

____

Begin to install them in you.

Have an accountability partner.

In the calendar, mark with green the days you implement the habit and in red, the days you don't.

See the result after 30 days.

Do not stop installing the 2 habits that you have chosen previously and jump to 2 other different habits after 30 days. Rather continue with the same in the second month and add one more habit that you need to install in yourself to create your destiny.   (Contd....)

Create an environment which supports your habit

Surround your- self with people who will motivate you and inspire you.

It's easier to form bad habits than good but that is not going to help you create your destiny.

Habits have types. There are habits based on our identity and personality. Habits based on our professions. Habits formed from our environment and family.

Habits are infectious. Make them your best friend. Live a life that is full of life. Throbbing with goodness and happiness.

21 DAY MYTH.

We have read or heard that it takes 21 days to implement a habit. It is not very easy to implement a habit in 21 days as it is generally believed. Research says that it takes 66 days on an average to build a habit.

Feel joy when you follow the habit even for a day. Appreciating and acknowledging ourselves is important.

Sometimes, when things don't go our way, we may get frustrated. But don't give up. Build resilience and start again.

The joy of finishing something is multifold than the joy when we started doing it. Experience the joy and you will never fail in continuing a habit.

List your challenges while installing a New Habit:

____

____

____

____

____

Challenges while implementing a Habit

- The adrenaline rush comes down drastically when we decide to continue to implement habits.

- Lack of self-motivation.

- Procrastination.

- Negative self-talk.

- External circumstances.

- Losing sight of the end goal.

How can you go from Habits to Destiny?

- Habits is your power-bank to fuel your destiny.

- Habits are proactive and within your control.

- Habits Empower

- A Habit formed never leaves you.

More Power to you my dear......................................

I am waiting to see you create your Destiny and be a game changer in your life.

THATHASTHU!   SO BE IT!   AMEN!

With Immense Love,

Kalyani.

9

CONSISTENCY

(Constant Delight!)

"Success isn't always about greatness. It's about consistency. Consistent hard work leads to success. Greatness will come."

— **Dwayne Johnson**

My Dearest ....,

Trust All is Well with you. You texted me saying that you have set actionable goals and have started to put them to action. Isn't that awesome?

ACTION – such a power packed word. It is dynamic. It is LIVE WIRE. It is in motion. It has an impact on us - mentally, emotionally, spiritually, physically and financially.

Actions are the only way which tells us our progress. Remember the saying, "An empty vessel makes more noise." Just saying out aloud your desires is not going to conjure up any magic unless you start acting on it.

We are all great starters. The enthusiasm, the adrenaline rush that we feel, when we want to do something is so infectious. But alas! We are not finishers.

Pause here and recall the number of times we started doing something, which we know is the right thing to do, but gave up mid- way. We did not reach the end line. Do you know why? What we lacked was CONSISTENCY.

Action without consistency will not give you any results. But right action with the consistent efforts will give you massive results.

Consistency is like exercise that needs to be done every day. Consistency does not just mean doing the same thing in the same way. Consistency in action means- you do not stop doing what needs to be done. You develop a mindset to break through all obstacles and have a do or die attitude. It is consistency which builds your tenacity for success. It makes you strong.

How can you be CONSISTENT in your Actions?

Remember, you are creating your own destiny and it's a powerful and empowering decision that you have taken. Bold, I would say. This will propel you to be consistent.

Keep being self-motivated.

Inspire yourself.

Place reminders. Appreciate yourself. Break tasks and make it measurable. Don't aim for perfection.

Do not over promise. Even to yourself. Use motivational tools to keep you going even if you don't feel like it. There will be many phases in our journey to our goal, when we feel like giving up. But it is precisely at this point that you don't give up. Don't give yourself any options. Do not procrastinate. There is no better time than NOW.

Your biggest enemy is Procrastination – i.e. postponing doing the inevitable. Understanding the enemy is important. For that;

1. Understand your mind-set.
2. List out the reasons why you procrastinate.

All the reasons can be reasoned out if you only knew why.

Is it fear, lack of knowledge, sheer laziness, lack of motivation, stuck in between not knowing where to go, lack of self-discipline or knowledge about your product or service, a sense of overwhelmingness and more?

Identify that. Once you identify and accept the real reason, you can start working on it.

How does Procrastination affect your end goal?

- It reduces your self-confidence
- Diverts your time in doing less important activities
- Reduces Enthusiasm in doing what you must do
- Delays end goal
- Creates dissatisfaction
- Creates anxiety and stress
- Self-loathing- because of your inability to do what you must be doing.
- Creates new challenges and obstacles
- Become an object of ridicule
- Lose faith in your capabilities and dream

Pressing the pause button is very important. For every step that you take, pause, and see if you are going the right way, or you have to course correct. Pausing is short term. Inner reflection. Whereas Procrastination is an outer, visible reflection of your capabilities.

Here is a small trick you must try out to cheat procrastination. I learnt it from the book 5 second rule by Mel Robbins.

"The 5 Second Rule is simple. If you have an instinct to act on a goal, you must physically move within 5 seconds, or your brain will kill it. The moment you feel an instinct or a desire to act on a goal or a commitment, use the Rule. When you feel yourself hesitate before doing something that you know you should do, count 5-4-3-2-1-GO and move towards action."

Implement this in even small areas in your life. For instance- In the morning, should you get up when you actually want to or snooze the alarm when it goes off? Don't think. Get up. Practice this for a few days. You must develop high resolve to achieve your dreams.

CONSISTENCY DOES NOT MEAN YOU WONT CHANGE AT ALL.

It means you will continue doing what needs to be done, to have the desired positive result. You will change where you need to bring about changes but keep going. You have to be unstoppable.

You have to develop your mindset to be consistent in your purpose, in your goals, in your thought and in your actions

Consistency and Persistence needs a little bit of positive stubbornness.

Stand your ground, close your ears to naysayers, review your actions and make changes wherever and whenever necessary.

It is not enough just to desire that you want to do something. It is important to fight for what you firmly believe in and want to do and stand up for yourself.

Consistency is far more powerful and rewarding than intensity. Consistency beats talent.

The personal tool for practicing consistency is Will Power.

Be Persistent.

Get organized and draw a ritual /routine calendar. Follow it, come what may. Do not allow your mind to talk to you. Which means, no dwelling on the thought of what you must do.

Develop Self-Control. Learn to say No to yourself. Be stubborn. Decide to shut your ears to all the inner negative words which fools you into loving a easy, lazy life. Self- control is strength. Use self-Awareness with it. Because self- Awareness is power.

Self-Control can be implemented in these areas

a. Body – Physical health and movements
b. Mind – Being aware of what you think and how you can use it as your friend
c. Emotions – How do you feel in undesirable situations and how you bounce back
d. Actions - How you do something and its impact around you and on yourself
e. Social – Do not get influenced by negative or external forces which do not help you.

Consistency is a combination of Hard-work and effort. It is loving yourself and life and a deep desire to create your destiny. It is respecting yourself at the highest level. Consistency is manic focus in action and not giving up no matter what. It is courage to fight against all obstacles that will come your way and you still push towards your goal. It is nature testing your resolve and determination.

"Daily, consistent, focused, faithful expectation raises the miracle power of achieving your dreams."

– John Di Lemme.

A common trait that all successful people share is consistency. Consistency in thought, words, action and desire.

You are your own sculptor, and your tools are in your hands - to create your own future. And I know you will pass this test of your will power in glowing colors.

Develop your consistency quotient. Consistency in action shapes your CHARACTER.

THATHASTHU!   SO BE IT!   AMEN!

With Immense Love,

Kalyani.

10

CHARACTER

(THE BEAUTIFUL SCULPTURE – THE YOU)

"Thoughts lead on to purposes; purposes go forth in actions; actions form habits; habits decide character; and character fixes our destiny."

— **Tryon Edwards**, American theologian

(1809 – 1894)

"Knowledge will give you power, but character respect."

- Bruce Lee

My dearest ....,

Bob Proctor said something I love. He said CHANGE IS INEVITABLE, BUT PERSONAL GROWTH IS A CHOICE. Our lives will always change. But our future is determined by our actions today.

The fifth law is Character.

"Character is repeated habits, and repeated habits alone can reform character" – Swami Vivekananda.

Habits build our character. Every act of ours define us. It defines our personality and sculpts our character. Unlike talents and gifts that are bestowed upon us by the Universe, our character is in our hands.

"Character is destiny," is a quote attributed to the Greek philosopher, Heraclitus. This quote implies that destiny, or fate, is not a predetermined outside force, but that one's future, or destiny, is determined by his own inner character.

"Character cannot be developed in ease and quiet. Only through experience of trial and suffering can the soul be strengthened, ambition inspired, and success achieved."

Helen Keller

Character is the sum total of mental and moral qualities distinctive to an individual. It is our character which makes each of us unique.

It takes vision, courage, perseverance, resilience, commitment, patience, hard work and industry to be a good starter and a good finisher. On the other hand, **impatience, laziness, procrastination and doubt** affect the end result of our destiny.

Character building is part of our lifestyle which defines us. The who we are every minute, every day without any external control or supervision is the true us. Sculpting our own character is a very conscious choice. Character is like a habit. It cannot change every day or minute.

DESTINY IS NOT AUTO DRIVEN BUT SELF-DRIVEN

There's no doubt that our character has a profound effect on our future. What we must remember, however, is not merely how powerful character is in influencing our destiny, but how powerful we are in shaping our own character and, therefore, our own destiny.

"When wealth is lost, nothing is lost; when health is lost, something is lost; when character is lost, all is lost."

- **Billy Graham**

Anne Frank, the 13-year-old victim of Nazi persecution said in her diary, "The formation of a person's character lies in their own hands." Though there will be influencers shaping our character when we are young, it is our responsibility to sculpt ourselves.

Thus, character is both formed and revealed by how one deals with everyday situations as well as extraordinary pressures and temptations. Like a well-made tower, character is built stone by stone, decision by decision.

"We all have these self-constructed personalities, and we believe that our likes and dislikes make up a strong part of our personality and who we are. But we can choose our own likes and dislikes. They don't have to just be automatic unconscious reactions."

– Todd Perelmuter

While character and personality are both used to describe a person's behavior, the two are different aspects of the individual. Personality of a person is instantly visible whereas character is visible only during challenging times or situations.

"Good character is not formed in a week or a month. It is created little by little, day by day. Protracted and patient effort is needed to develop good character."

- Heraclitus

There are thousands of personality tests but hardly any character tests. Have you ever thought about that?

The 6 pillars of Character

1. BEING HUMANE— Kindness, Compassion, Love, Tolerance, Acceptance

2. INTEGRITY — Self-Respect, Respect for others, Loyalty, Honesty, Reliable.

3. RESPONSIBILITY — Duty, Accountability, Pursuit of excellence, social responsibility towards community.

4. FAITH – Faith in oneself, in the Divine, in society and loved ones, Trust

5. SPIRITUALITY – Soul-Building, respecting all religions, looking inwards.

6. SELF-REALISATION – Self-Awareness, Self-Introspection, Desire to better ones-self each day.

"Dreams are the touchstones of our character."

- Henry David Thoreau

Character building is a continuous process. Many aspects in our life influence our character. Environment, family, friends, childhood, society, the words that we hear every day, our lifestyle, friends, education and social media. But the choice to shape ourselves is ours. No two people, brought up in the same way are similar. Siblings are as different as day and light.

Character is inbuilt and part of our karma. I like to call character as SWABHAVA- the power to create our own Avatar. It is about constantly looking inward – observing ourselves and recreating our thoughts and installing new habits and improving ourselves every day.

A character is like a lighthouse. A character is so fragile and strong at the same time. It can be tarnished in seconds and torn to shreds in minutes. Or it stands the test of time. We need to guard our character with our strength of diligence and wisdom. Our sterling qualities which shine out should not be sullied by external influences.

"Just as we develop our physical muscles through overcoming opposition - such as lifting weights - we develop our character muscles by overcoming challenges and adversity."

- Stephen Covey

Character and Personality should not clash. Our body language, the words we use, the way we dress, the work we do, the friends we keep, the daily habits and rituals that we follow- designs our character.

We are a combination of positive and negative qualities. While we are born with certain characteristics, it is possible to cultivate our character with self-reflection and effort. With the thoughts you had on creating your destiny, you worked on your words and actions and habits – creating the character that you are now. And with this transformation, your destiny is now real.

Build your character every day. People with strong character show compassion, are honest and fair, display self-discipline in setting and meeting goals, make good judgments, show respect to others, stand up for their beliefs, have a strong sense of responsibility, are good citizens who are concerned for their community, maintain self-respect, and are happy individuals.

The great philosopher Aristotle believed that character helped explain a person's past actions and could predict future behaviour.

Character is predictable.

It doesn't change.

To be a true to oneself, one needs to develop a solid character which will stand the test of all trials and challenges. To be a self-leader, without a title, your character will be your armour and will protect you from all negative forces. You will shine bright wherever you are.

What you are now and what do you want to be? Self - introspect and look deep within yourself with all honesty. Self -Awareness is directly connected to sculpting your character which will lead to self-realization and thus help in creating your own destiny.

The following principle from Patanjali's Yoga Sutras is very interesting: "For the repelling of unwholesome thoughts, their opposites should be cultivated. Unwholesome thoughts, such as harming someone and so forth—whether done, caused to be done, or approved, whether arising from greed, anger or infatuation, whether mild, moderate or extreme — never cease to ripen into ignorance and suffering. Therefore, one must cultivate their opposites."

List down the areas of where you need to grow and build your character:

____

____

____

____

____

____

____

____

____

How can we change our character and transform ourselves?

- Know your weakness and where you need to change and why
- Accept and believe that you can change
- Know why that change is important to your personal and professional growth.

How will Character building help you in creating your own destiny?

1. Self-Actualisation
2. Sticking to your goals
3. Sustaining the enthusiasm that you started out with and Perseverance.
4. Solving inner conflicts and surmounting challenges and sudden twists which will come your way.
5. Humility and Gratitude

Every word you speak, your actions reflect your character.

My Dear........................., It is your character which will help you sustain your Destiny that you create.

REFLECTIONS

Reflect on what is your character?

My Ideal Characteristics:

____

____

____

____

____

____

____

____

____

Character is complete and conscious transformation of the self. It is practicing and preaching what you say and do. It is the biggest tool for self-transformation, where you meet your ideal self to create your deserved Destiny.

My dear............................., You Deserve to live the life of your choice, your Dreams.

THATHASTHU!   SO BE IT!   AMEN!

With Immense Love,

Kalyani.

11

TRANSFORMATION

(Birth of The New YOU)

"It is not until you change your identity to match your life blueprint that you will understand why everything in the past never worked."

– Shannon L. Alder

My Dearest ....,

The journey has been quite interesting, sharing my thoughts to such a smart and talented person as you. I really appreciate your patience in implementing all that we have shared here.

I can see the transformation in you. Transformation is not just physical. It is a transformation of the soul. It is so visible and full of bursting energy. It is palpable. For transforming ourselves, creating a new you, you need immense **Self-Love**. It is not unusual to realize that many of us do not love ourselves. The question that we need to ask ourselves is 'Why? If we need to love ourselves, who would we want to be.

Self-transformation is to transcend from what you were to what you want to be, and where you want to be. Creating your own destiny means transforming and giving birth to a new you and to sculpt your own life. It's a popular observation that what got you until here today, may not take you to your future destination tomorrow. If you are the vehicle that is traveling the path to your intended destiny, are you fit for the road?

The self-transformation of you as a person and your core self-identity, therefore, has to mirror the chosen path of your destiny. It will be a constant process of evaluating your inner-self, your value-system, beliefs, actions, habits, character-traits, personality, external associations and manifestations, in the light of your intended and defined road to your destiny.

Every known demand or expectation, as with every unexpected twist, turn and obstacle on that road, needs a check and POSITIVE EVOLUTION (not mere adaptation) of your identity, character and personality, towards your better and evolved self. Not surprisingly, the end-product of yourself at the finish-line of your destiny might look radically different, from the you the person when you began the journey of taking your dreams to your destiny!

You overcame all challenges and over-rode all obstacles to reach your destination. You transformed your weaknesses, built on your strengths and created your destiny.

You wrote to me about the steps that you took for your Self-transformation:

- Observing yourself and identifying the gaps in your qualities that you needed for your personal growth.
- Consciously avoid destructive patterns.
- Cultivate traits to sustain the transformation process. Keep growing.
- Training yourself to push your limits and reach your milestones.
- Developing a strong mind-set.
- Freeing yourself from compulsive behaviours and attitudes.
- Learning new skills and working hard on yourself.
- Align and build your character to fulfil your Destiny.
- Using your POWER OF CHOICE.

It is awesome that you chose to exercise your power of choice. Most of us do not realize the personal weapon that we all possess which no one can take away from us.

Essentially, Transformation is an extreme, radical change. Self -Transformation is the true test of creating our own identity, personality and character

I also believe in this age of Free Will which describes our capacity to make choices that are genuinely our own. With free will comes moral responsibility and personal accountability – our ownership of our good and bad deeds.

Like eating, going to the bathroom, or exercising, self-transformation cannot be delegated.

In the powerful book **MAN'S SEARCH FOR MEANING**, Holocaust survivor and psychiatrist Viktor Frankl observes that, "Everything can be taken from a man but one thing: the last of the human freedoms — to choose one's attitude in any given set of circumstances, to choose one's own way." Even when life deals us a horrible hand, "Every human being has the freedom to change at any instant."

"As long as you are alive, you will either live to accomplish your own goals and dreams or you will be used as a resource to accomplish someone else's goals and dreams".

Grant Cardone

Author and motivational speaker

"You are not the victim of the world, but rather the master of your own destiny. It is your choices and decisions that determine your destiny."

-Roy T Bennett

"It is not until you change your identity to match your life blueprint that you will understand why everything in the past never worked."

– Shannon L. Alder

To experience complete transformation, you should be healed from past hurts, disappointments, abuses and failures.

I would suggest you try this wonderful technique called Ho'opponono - a Hawaiin technique.

According to the Hawaiian practices, we have a spiritual body, mental body and an emotional body, that are all a part of our physical body. We are all at different stages. The art of Ho'oponopono is to connect the three minds and process in healing the world by healing oneself

What is Ho'oponopono?

Ho'oponopono means 'to make things right'. It is a prayer and a Hawaiian practice for forgiveness. It is a powerful mantra for giving you a clean slate.

A mantra of four affirmations:
- **I am sorry**
- **Forgive me**
- **Thank you**
- **I love you**

"Transformation is not five minutes from now; it's a present activity. In this moment you can make a different choice, and it's these small choices and successes that build up over time to help cultivate a healthy self-image and self-esteem."

Jillian Michaels

"Every success story is a tale of constant adaption, revision and change."

- Richard Branson

The Ho'oponopono healing comes in 4 basic steps:

1. I'm Sorry

Saying sorry and admitting responsibility is the first part of the healing in Ho'oponopono.

'I am responsible for anything that has ever happened to me, or anything wrong that I've witnessed.'

The first step is just about **accepting the fact that all the wrong things started within you**.

2. Forgive me

Say, *'Please forgive me'*. It is a form of asking an apology from the universe, it doesn't matter that you have wronged or not, it is a cleansing method that removes negativity. Asking for forgiveness is a healing method in Ho'oponopono that helps you **move on in life**.

3. Thank you

Keep saying thank you repetitively. Gratitude towards the universe is an important part of the healing process in Ho'oponopono. Saying thank you for all the forgiveness, thank you for all the change within you, thanks to yourself for being who you are. ***Gratitude is a powerful emotion and must be said again and again to bring in the fresh air of positivity.***

4. I love you

Say I love you to yourself, to god, to your body, to the sheltering house you live in, to your surroundings. Love is a powerful emotion, with love comes layers of warmth and security. ***Giving love is a caring and affectionate emotion that accelerates the healing process*** in Ho'oponopono.

Power of Ho'oponopono

Repeating the Ho'oponopono mantra allows deeper concentration. Repetition of Ho'oponopono also allows reprogramming of the subconscious mind for better healing. When you feel sorry, thank you and love deeply it helps you get rid of the clogs within you. The process gives in lots of positive energies. It helps in better understanding of your inner- self when felt enchanting Ho'oponopono.

The most important journey you will take in your life will usually be the one of Self- Transformation. Often, this is the scariest because it requires the greatest changes, in your life.

How can you continue your Self- Transformation journey? Your story is now known to the world. Your life-story will be an example of grit and determination, of self-love and humility, of courage and compassion.

- Read
- Have a mentor to guide you
- Share your knowledge and skills
- Give before you receive
- Practice affirmations
- Love yourself in every way
- Take care of your health – Mentally, Physically and Emotionally
- Be Money-wise
- Have enriching Relationships with the people you meet. Weed out those who stand in your way to achieving your Destiny
- Say No to yourself and others if it does not serve your purpose
- Think Noble thoughts

- Practice Humility.

- Be Grateful

- Pray

Having Gratitude is a virtue. Feel Grateful for everything in your life. Positive and negative experiences, the good and the not so good people you encounter. The more you are grateful for, the more things will happen in your life, that you will feel grateful.

Every person that we meet is a teacher. We need to go through the bad, to realise what is good. What goes around, comes around.

I want to end by saying that "THE ATTITIDE OF GRATITUDE IS YOUR ALTITUDE". And I am so grateful to you, my dearest .... that you took the time out to read and act on some of the points discussed in this book. And yes, I will soon be sharing with you the 'Eight Self-Transformation Traits' in my next book.

Turn the next page and write your own Destiny.

THATHASTHU!   SO BE IT!   AMEN!

With Immense Love,

Kalyani.

12

DESTINY

(Sum Total of all our Choices)

"Destiny is not a matter of chance, it is a matter of choice; it is not a thing to be waited for, it is a thing to be achieved."

— William Jennings Bryan

WRITE YOUR OWN DESTINY

____

____

____

____

____

____

____

____

____

____

THATHASTHU!   SO BE IT!   AMEN!